HOMAGE

Mícheál Fanning

salmonpoetry

Published in 2006 by
Salmon Poetry Ltd.,
Cliffs of Moher, County Clare, Ireland
Website: www.salmonpoetry.com
email: info@salmonpoetry.com

ISBN 1 903392 49 7

Cover artwork: Brenda Friel
Cover design & typesetting: Siobhán Hutson

Acknowledgements

Special thanks to Aogán Ó Muircheartaigh, Pádraig Ó Snodaigh & Coiscéim, *The Kerryman*, *An Sagart*, *Lá* and *Ildána*.

Contents

Introduco
Homage To Our Times

Between reading,
discourses in praise of our ancestors
and spells when I walk for hours,
I observe the falcon — like a kite's suspension —
with outspread wings.

We have the present,
glimpses of the past
and the dreamy future
in the epiphany of Time.

The sun illuminates the island view
and morning advances.

Man–Woman

Primates appear, the great ice age covers and snaps.
Ground/man formed by the wind howling
from the soul of God.
Woman taken out of man and vice versa.

"I believe in the unity of the opposites.
Everything is flux," says Heraclitus.

Charles Darwin

Noah sailed and lived with his menagerie
on board the Ark.

And Charles Darwin kept carrier, runt, fantail, barb,
pouter, jacobin, and trumpeter pigeons on *HMS Beagle*,

all revert to ancestral characters.
Dream we did of another world.

Hominids walk upright
in Tanzania two million years ago.

Homo habilis uses tools in Ethiopia
and reaches China.

Homo sapiens settles in Neanderthal
uses flint tools and explores the world.

Homo sapiens sapiens reaches Australia,
America and Pakistan, populates the planet.

Goats and horses are seen
at Lascaux, Altamira and Sahara.

I saw hunters with bows and spears
painted on rock in caves near Maputo.

Carnac stones mark the holy place
and happy summer holidays in Brittany.

Family Holiday in Egypt

Huge pyramids constructed.
The leader's final journey
to The Valley of the Kings takes 70 days.

Food, drink and *The Book of the Dead*
to sustain a pharaoh's last itinerary.
To be reborn and rule once again.

My wife Nóirín, daughter Ruth,
and son Peter
saw the Colossi at Thebes–Luxor,

and with them, later,
I visited the pyramids and the colossal sphinx
at Giza, hieroglyphics carved in stone.

Gilgamesh was published
in Sumer
on cuneiform tablets.

Life flourishes in Sargon's empire
between the Tigris and Euphrates
in Babylon and Mesopotomia.

Palaeolithic hunters and gatherers provide.
People of the Neolithic with their hand-hoe till crops
on the banks of the Boyne, bury their dead in cairns
and we sing the descant of Co. Meath.

Dream

So a rainbow arched across the firmament
as Abraham, the hundred-year old shepherd, prepared
to offer up Isaac, a gift from nonagenarian Sarah.
She had remained barren until later life.

Rebecca watered Isaac's camels.
Jacob worked for fourteen years to win Rachel
and limping Jacob, now named Israel, dreamed
pictures from the other world.

One time I dreamed of a stairway
reaching from earth to heaven,
traversed by shining golden angels
and another time by waifs, ogres and demons.

Sailing on The Nile

Moses led them, those of descent by natural selection,
from North Africa.
Change is slow. The more we know — we realize —
we are more ignorant.

We toiled near Aswan,
sailed fellucas on the Nile,
but for my son and daughter I feared,
as they haggled with taxi drivers close to Cairo.

The cloud rested over the camp by day
and a fire burned over it by night.
We brought the body of the dreamer, Joseph, with us
and the rainbow bowed from heaven to earth.

Visit to Syria

Who is involved with our waking,
eating, thinking, lovemaking, coffee making,
sleeping and dreaming?

Consecrate us not to despair.
Whisper our worries into the goat's ears
and drive him into the desert.

Descent occurs with modification
through natural selection, instinct occurred
by slow accumulation of profitable variations.

The wolf-dog doesn't walk a straight line,
the strongest live, and the weakest die.
The Syrians surprise the Rameses at Kadesh.

Phoenicians' star rises. Hittites collapse without the help
of the Ugarit. Nóirín, Peter, Ruth, Rachel and I
walked the orange grove village in Syria. More later.

The Mortal Immortals

Our father sent fire and an epidemic
to punish his flock.
A great stream of water gushed out of the rock.

A plague killed 14,700. Take the fire-pans,
beat them into plates to cover the altar.
Aaron stood between the dead and the living,
    so that we may not falter.

The earth opened and swallowed the dissident families.
The mortal immortals went down as fireflies to the world
    of the dead unrequited.
Our mother put a bronze snake on a pole for those bitten
    to behold.
Partake of a tortilla in Le Pans' Homely Household.

Anxiety and Restoration

Throw the gold bull-calf into the fire
and ascend the fire-mountain again.

Obey our father and mother
and they will bless your towns and fields,

bless your corn crops and the food you prepare from them
and if you don't — you will find no peace anywhere:

no place to call your own
and eat the bread of suffering.

You will be overwhelmed with anxiety, hopelessness and despair.
I am addicted to Courtney's bread, Murphy's and Sheehy's
    icecream.

Every morning you will wish for evening, and every evening you
will wish for morning and you will be sent bound in ships
    into exile.

But I am restored and blessed by Mossie and Joe, guardians
    of the peace
because I turned back to my father and mother with all my heart.

Rameses II constructs Abu Simbel. Pharaoh sits on his throne.
Thanks to Lucas, Urs, Sophia and Joan we wear masks
with Aigedlige Clique, and again become unknown.

We All Fall Down 6

The Walls fell.
They all fell.
Jericho fell.

12,000 people of Ai killed in one day.
People of Gibeon enslaved,
forced to cut wood and carry water.

Offer thanksgiving morning, noon and night to
the Almighty. "As for my family and me,
we will serve Him and His Queen."
Ring a Rosy.
We all fall down.

Disloyal

Jael crushed Sisera's skull
with hammer and tent-peg. Plonk.
And there was peace for forty years.

Gideon blew trumpets
and broke jars. Crash.
120,000 Midianites slaughtered.

The concubine from Bethlehem was dissected
into twelve pieces. Slit, gash and slash.
At Gibeah 25,000 massacred.

There was no law and order at that time. Wrangle and smother.
Everyone did as they pleased. I am disloyal to my Abuna.
May I understand, repent and turn to you again, mother?

Loyalty   8

for Ruth while studying in Monastery of San Nicoló, The Lido, Venice

Ruth remembered Naomi's sons, Mahlon
and Chilion, and was still in love with the dead
as she toiled in the barley fields.

And loyal Ruth you knew love
so much,
as you loved the almost impossible —

you loved dead Mahlon dearly
and so you married Boaz after all these years.
David was yet to be conceived.

Ruth, three thousand one hundred years later,
Karol Wojtyla lifted you over the praying
Welsh crowds in the Pontcanna fields.

Abigail & David

Abigail bowed to David
and threw herself on the ground
at David's feet.

I bring you two hundred loaves of bread,
five roasted sheep, ten stone of roasted grain,
a hundred bunches of grapes,

two hundred cakes of dried figs
and two leather bags full of wine
to give to your men. Eat, drink and be merry.

David, appointed
through Samuel
after the fall of tall and moody Saul,

you stand on the boundaries of the spirit-dream world
betwixt our fathers, our mothers
and on the boundaries of sanity and compassion.

And yours like ours is not a life of peace
as you hide from danger after danger, year after year.
Take cover, lie low and go to ground.

Mary Garvey, Bríd Pat Moriarty, John Martin and
Séamus Kennedy — dip the sheep and milk the cows.
Pádraig Ó Siochrú, round Coláiste Íde walk the hound.

The Assyrians replenish their stables
with a hundred horses a day in their cosmic fight with evil.
Empires loot, grow in leaps and bounds.

David

David lamented after Saul and Jonathan.
For forty years David ruled, troubled by his own family wars,
civil wars and wars foreign on the Zion continent.

Nathan chides David. Do not covet Bathsheba.
Do not murder Uriah. *"You are that man."*
David repents. Bathsheba bears Solomon.

Absalom rebels, is defeated and killed.
David went on up to the Mount of Olives
weeping. Sooner or later we all weep.

Mother and sisters reach down from above and take hold of him.
The mother alone is his defence in David's city.
He listens to my cry for help. Our father and mother love and live.

Ashurnasirpal reigns supreme in Assyria.
Zhou overthrows Shang dynasty in China.
Daniel Day-Lewis boxes. Ultimately we all sleep.

Solomon's 700 Princesses
& 300 Concubines

Solomon constructed
the splendid temple
in the city of his father, David.

Wise Solomon built the temple with cedar
and pines in the united Israelite kingdom,
four hundred and eighty years after the exodus.

Huram decorated with bronze artefacts
a majestic temple,
for our Abba to live in and to house

the two stone tablets of Moses in the Covenant Box,
over which hung the cloud shining
with the dazzling light of the Lord's presence.

Wise as he was, Solomon was attracted to his seven hundred
princesses whom he married and to his three hundred
concubines. The scrapper Tom Cruise claims —

our women — ah they do —
sustain us. Israelites kill 100,000 Syrians.
Elijah is taken up to Heaven.

Wind is the air in motion.
The winds of change
whistle where they blow.

Wind causes currents off Inch Strand
effects the movement of the waters
and tides fall and rise in the blue ocean.

The Discourse of Mr. Poeta Paris

CALL TO HELEN

Paris thanks her for the amity —
only for the ears of the angels in paradise.
They threw him into disarray
because of love or infatuation.
Athena and Hera disregarded;
Aphrodite demanded it, this amatory.

PROVIDENTIA

Paris heard her call across
the boreal wind.

Eternity is on their side
to understand hate, love and resipiscence.
"The rules of love are set in place."
The dark curtain falls peremptorily.
Priam's son and Zeus' daughter
step favourably, in magic readiness
for their animated journeys.

I leave you, Helen, for Oenone.
Good providence to you and Menelaus.
Let's not rail against but entreat our gods
for restraint. Fairuz, sing for Val and Marian.
The Chieftains sing "Sé mo Laoch".
God and Mary bless you, in Kilkenny...

Achilles & Briseis (c. 800 B.C.)

Briseis of the winds, you hear Achilles' storm,
entropy of frenetic gales fills a golden sail.
Come about, run the wind, reach the port
and catch the sudden gust of wind.

Achilles, you reach the port ahead of time,
mentor maritime.
Who cares about Paris,
Helen and Troy?

Briseis, Achilles knows that you come
from the ship-kissed shores
and long-backed Agamemnon desires
you on the sun-drenched coast.

A hundred black ships ride on course.
Foundling Briseis of the caves,
you ride the storm alectory, where the
sea breathes you, heaves, roams and supports.

You, Briseis, you kiss Achilles' body
with such care. Gusts grow where Briseis
and red-haired Achilles
run the gilded seas to shell-song shores.

Our Daughters Scream

But Elijah, Elisha and now Isaiah
call in vain.
War ensues between Israel and Moab.

Hazael smothered
Syria's king
with a blanket soaked in water.

Then the angel went to the Assyrian camp
and killed 185,000 sons.
Our daughters yowl and holler.

The fall of Samaria, 722 — one hundred and thirty
years of humiliation, and in 586, the fall of Jerusalem.
The people of Judah were driven into Babylonia.

Our Days

O King David, demiurge,
soldier of Saul, for forty-seven years,
harper and psalmist of Jebus, par excellence, help.

Our days are like a passing shadow,
we pass through life like exiles and strangers
and we cannot escape death and rot.

Praise, eat, drink
and dance in the presence
of our *Faeder.*

Shout with joy to the sound of trumpets,
horns, cymbals and harps.
Vindicate us our *fader and mater.*

Go hear the National Foresters' Band play
in John Murphy's, and The Madagascar Trio
in Pádi Brosnan's. March round the town with
The Dingle Fife & Drum and T.F. Meagher's.

Solomon & Socrates

Solomon ruled supreme for twenty years
and built the temple,
the kingdom splintered amongst fears.

Half a million of North Israel's
best soldiers lay dead.
Zedekiah lost his confidence.

Nebuchadnezzar of Babylonia burned the temple down.
It lay desolate for seventy years.
Anointed Cyrus proclaimed the rise of Persia.

Ugly pug-faced, snub-nosed Socrates
knew by dialectical dialogue
that he didn't know anything.

He questioned the uncertain world —
the soul alone is incorruptible
and indestructible.

Odysseus
for Michael Gibbons

I am the famous warrior.
My kind father, Laertes,
waits for me at the spring of Olympus.

Penelope, my loyal wife, is stranded many miles
from here. My son, bold Telemachus,
rows and reaches in triremes across the seas.

We wait, we wait, wait. I am famous
for waiting, marking time!
We sail into the harbours of Alexandria.

We wait at Thonis.
I fear that emotion more than a fight
with Polyphemus. We wait.

O Ezra, our father, write prayers in Aramaic,
play the cymbals and shofar
and proclaim our hope and faith.

Greek peasants repel Persians at Marathon.
Miltiades won on the fateful day
and held the sway in 490 against Darius.

Sophocles won renowned prizes
for scapegoats — blind Oedipus,
his Jocasta and loyal Antigone.

The Greeks wore masks on stage.
Spartans spared the city as Athenian
women sang Euripides's Electra.

Leonidas stood bravely at Thermopylae.
Themistocles built 200 triremes
and beat the Persians at Salamis in 480.

Orestes & Hermione

for Don and Mary-Susan

Orestes awakes in the star-filled morning.
A falling star for his love, Hermione.

The Plough winks. Orestes walks along a
cow-track to where Hermione laughs in love.

They romp along
the sky-track to Sirius.

There is only gala for Hermione, his love,
on the ylem-path to Pleiades.

Orion guides them on
the salamander-strand to Pegasus.

Orestes and Hermione chant
Love's magical songs together.

NOTE:
Orestes, Agamemnon and Clytemnestra's son, expresses love
for his betrothed, Hermione, Helen and Menelaus' daughter.

Plato's Echoes & Shadows

for those under my medical care

Nehemiah, the wine servant, mourned for all.
Artaxerxes approved his request
to return home to rebuild the city wall.

We confess our troubles to our Abuna above.
Spare us because of your great love, O sisters and brothers,
how glorious and terrifying is the Word.

All we hear are echoes
and all we see are shadows
housed in our vulnerable bodies.

Soul is the higher and permanent form.
In my happy and glorious football teens
I reflected on Plato in St.Brendan's, Killarney.

Mr Cogito

THALES thought it was
the water element.

ANAXIMANDER made the first map.
"The earth hangs unsupported in space," he said.

ZENO's tortoise outpaces Achilles, thus
proving that logical argument can be faulty.

DEMOCRITUS saw the world cannot be cut
and change was casual.

EMPEDOCLES substantiates all
as earth, water, air and fire.

God is a mathematician — the goat-bearded PYTHAGORAS
thought and mathemathical order pervaded the world.

The poet XENOPHANES said all was a woven web of guesses
and that the gods were what you wanted them to be

but his pupil, PARMENIDES, said everything was
imperishable. All is one.

This is the earth —
above — the upper stratosphere…and the atmosphere
the Hydrosphere bathes us

the Lithosphere is what we touch
and the barysphere — centre of our earth — where we journey.

Solemn ERATOSTHENES, librarian at Alexandria,
looked at the sun over his head

in Aswan and Alexandria
and measured the world's circumference.

Woman and Man are the measure of all things —
PROTAGORAS, the famous sophist, thought.

Good old SOCRATES strove
to his self be true
the higher power is what we should know.

Soul is divine — PLATO thought
and ARISTOTLE knows.

Esther & Plato

Xerxes condemned his wife Vashti
into subordination and appointed a beautiful girl
of good figure, Esther, to be Queen.

O Mordecai, you understood beauty, intelligence,
government and prayer and interceded with Esther.
Bend low and bow to the love unseen

that we may celebrate for the sake of love.
Our enemies cast lots, Purim,
to determine the day to destroy us.

Haman hanged from a gallows twenty-two metres high,
    defamed,
built at his own house by his own orders, proclaimed,
to annihilate the Jews. Haman, the prosecutor, profaned.

Knowledge grows through critical argument
thought Plato in his academy and life is a theorem of
mathematical order

but points to higher things.
Intellect should control passions
through the will, as do philosopher kings.

I hope that you didn't miss HUUN HUUR TU
sing deep from their voice boxes in the Hillgrove.
Tadhg wasn't there to hear Roby Lakatos charm the
audience in the Skellig.

Job

Job, as good a man
as the world ever bore
and built a bridge of tears.

Job lost his seven sons, 7,000 sheep, 3,000 camels
and 1,000 cattle. Eliphaz, Bildad, Zophar and Elihu
condemned him as a diffident wretch.

But Job protested his innocence to his Elfader,
who never forgot and who created the sun, sky, snow, the seas,
the storms, the stars, Leviathan and the monster Behemoth.

What hope is there for me, O my sisters,
but to repent in ashes and dust and
speak the truth that withstands the test?

But Job was blessed and he loved long enough
to see his grand-children and great grand-children
and prospered more than ever.

David Sings

for Pádi & Máire Ó Sé and family

David the singer, harpist, knew
the ordinances of the Sun
which furnaces day in, day out.

He understood the tenets of the Law
but was exhausted by civil and external wars,
family feuds and attempted assassinations.

He confessed his sins to be righteous.
He understood the anguish, despair and the glory
of man who trusted his father and mother.

Be glad, birds of the morning, sea and mountains.
Praise my soul. To you alone,
to you alone sing — our love is eternal.

Your word is a lamp to guide me.
Gather the harvest of new potatoes with joy.
Live together in harmony.

Place a sentry at the door of my lips,
but only to praise in Cillmaolcéadair
and pay homage to Tom and Marie O'Connor.

Thanks to you Seán and Paddy Uí Mhathúna in Ballyhay, Paddy
Flannery and Peter Hand for the wild salmon, fresh cod, sceálta,
roguery, sole and filleted haddock from oceans of laughter.

"You are all Gods, you are sons and daughters
of the most high. Alleluia, Alleluia,"
and our *aldur*-Father's love is thunderous and pelagic.

Aristotle

If you are in a hurry to become rich
you set a trap for yourself. Adultery is on the way
to the world of the dead and is the short cut to death.
Your money can be gone in a flash.

Ants, rock-badgers,
lizards and locusts
are small
but very wise.

Aristotle, a doctor's son,
studied in Plato's academia. For ten years
kept his feet on the ground —
father of logic and anatomy.

Aristotle says that the real point
of anything is what it does —
a doctor healing,
a poet making poems and a priest praying.

But Aristotle understood logos
physics, logic, ethics,
biology, physiology,
material, efficient, formal and final causes.

Aristotle said man and woman cannot live alone —
praised poetics,
poetic tragedy and
the evocation of pity and fear.

The august polymath, Aristotle, tutored Alexander,
the exalted world conqueror, who
founded his library at Alexandria.
"Know your world," taught Aristotle.

Alexander who established the polis worldwide would wish
to be Diogenes — for him — social conventions false,
the cosmopolitan, the barrel-man barks, bites and snarls.
Perplexed Alexander never did come out of an alcohol coma.

670 Steps for Fulfilment 2 1

for Frank O'Connor

The silver chain will snap and
the golden lamp will fall and break.
Obey our immortal spirit's commands,
for this is what we were all created.

The wind blows south, blows north, round
and round and back again over The Skelligs.
We draw our breaths. Through stones and water we wade.
Our *beaupere* is our judge. Our mothers aid.

We hear and see the miracle of 60,000 pairs of gannets
chatter on Skellig Bheag. There is something greater than me —
the 1500 years of the mystery of Skellig Michael, the rocks,
Catherine's Manx shearwater and the furious unfurling sea.

Neoplatonist Plotinus saw the soul
as the ideal form. For something to be created
is for it to be thought for atonement.
We ascend 670 steps for fulfilment.

Friga

Friga walked barefoot
on her sea-water bubbling sands.
That was her niche
in *Ginnungapap*.
Friga struck a fair bargain in her
Valhalla
close to the Nordic sea.
Odin didn't ask for the impossible —
Hvergemir,
only *deus ex machina*.

But it's auspicious for her
absolved in Asgard.
Odin kissed her golden hair
and not again,
Friga, *bel esprit*,
until the Ragnarok.

NOTES (IN NORDIC MYTHOLOGY):
Odin and Friga were man and wife. Odin created the world from the
giant Ymir. He also created Ask and Embla, the first man and woman.
Ginnungapap: Yawning void.
Hvergemir: Well of life.
Ragnarok: The last day, the day of Reckoning.

Larkery

The winter cold is flown away
the summer sun warms,
light easterly breeze, blue skies.
Love's old ghosts visit.

The treasure of our love is as famous
as Solomon's for his lover
among the vineyards and hills.

I offer you wild flowers from Castlegregory,
purple fox-glove, orange woodbine, wild iris, fern and fuchsia
where — an exultation of wild larks is heard in the larkery.

Sun shines on us, souls that journey
on the golden sands. We recover.
Be circumspect about erotic love.

Lucretius praises Venus, the goddess of sexual love,
love and live unknown. Liadáin, Fergal, Marike and
Lorcán sing song of songs in the larkery, darlings.

Beatrice took Dante to the tenth heaven.
The Eternal Light touched his mind
so that Holy writ will heal the love-craven.

And so daring Dante did speak so kind.
Virgil led him round this place of Love. Beatrice
sang *"Te Deum"* for man and womankind.

Unexpected Peace

for Paula, Síle, Olga, Úna and members of Medaction Éire

We are overcome and in grave grief
but our hopeless situation is resolved.
A great light appears,
eternal light, prince of knowledge.

"But nothing is, everything is becoming," thought Plato.
Epicurus wrote — Live together non-violently.
The Epicurean encouraged — Enjoy life, live today.
The skull, our *memento mori*, recalls our mortality.

Pyrrho, sceptic that he was, realised that all knowledge
was conflicting, 'tis good we suspend our judgements.
We are the atoms of Democritus
celebrating in the glory of unexpected peace, mother.

Wolves and sheep will live together
in peace. Comfort, my people.
I am the one who saves you.
Come back to me, my children.

Our vigorous Brother is come.
Shout and sing, my sister Lysistrata!
Sing heavens. Shout for joy, earth.
Let the mountains burst into song.

Hear Danú play and sing in Pádi Ó Sé's. Peadar Ó Riada,
Cór Cúil Aodha, Eoin Duignan, Pendred Finbar and
the Quare Fellas sang there also. Then onto Altan in
Ionad an Bhlascaoid and later on in John Benny's and
the Droichead.

Who is lonelier than Jeremiah?
One disaster follows another.
The whole country is left in ruins.

My heart is crushed and I lament.
I wish my head were a well of water
and my eyes a fountain of tears.

Israel has fallen in 722
and Judah will fall in 587.
We are doomed.

We reject the Good.
We will be brought to trial
and put to shame.

What an uncertain man I am, O Jeremiah, though
why was I born? To end my life in disgrace?
Assist me in the unrest, O woman of the tears.

But you, my mater, will restore me after the seventy years
of lamentation and have mercy on every family
when we return home from our place of inglorious renewal.

We listen to Arabesque and K-Groove play Arabic and orient
dance-music. Ali Halimeh, Rifat Iqbal and Dominic Murray
speak to the backdrop of Jerusalem, the eternal city, exhibition.
Máirtín Ó Muilleoir and Bruce Kent care and Nuzha charm
    and palliate.

The Lament

Listen to my groans, mother.
I am held in utter contempt.

I have fallen into lonesome ways.
I am exhausted from loneliness.

I have forgotten what laughter is
and I'm fevered and delirious.

There is no salvation, I think.
I will never remember happiness again.

And I lament day and night, season
into season, year after year.

Is there no limit to your anger?
My father, have you rejected us forever?

We who are of this bodily world
aspire to citizenship of the holy city.

We, Tarantino gangsters, will get up again
and petition my sweetest friend.

Give us the will to live. Restore our
inner peace. Bring us back to you, Father.

Lacrimosa dies illa.
We lament, mother.

Ezekiel & Augustine

I, Ezekiel, saw a man sitting on a throne,
above the dome of dazzling crystal.
He shone all over with rainbow colours —
the dazzling light of the Abba's presence.

The four-headed creatures — Lion, human, bull, eagle —
underneath the dome,
darted to and fro with the speed of lightning
in all directions in Narnia, close to copper mines in Killarney.

Augustine married Plato and Christ, he confessed —
our lives are predestined, souls damned in anxiety.
The women's soprano songs return to the temple.
His intervention and grace lead to salvation in the
    City dormitory.

Daniel & Aquinas

Daniel dreams —
the fourth beast rises up against the one
who has been living forever. Jerusalem
is captured. Howl in grief, sister, brother.

Aquinas says the soul is known by its acts
but saw the heavenly light of Aristotle:
our motherfather, in pure existence.
We pay homage to the immortal spirit of our father.

Walk to Spillane's in Maharees.
Talk with T.P. and Normán i mBaile 'n Gall.
In Anascaul discourse with Francis Falvey.

Travel from O'Dowds or Mullalys
over Brandon to the Walshs, Bóthar.
Visit Dalys or Ashes in Camp and on to Mother.

Lament for a Palestinian —
Boy of Barja, 586 B.C. (Jan. 2 1998)

A bearded militia-man in a combat outfit
lifts a nine-year old child.
The child is dressed
in a simple jumper, pulled up a little
to show his girth of stomach
and bellybutton.
The fat child is motionless,
his long-jeaned pants
right trousers leg rolled up to his knees
barefoot, when he ran on the streets of Barja.
The child has deplorable head wounds.
The child is dead.
Our mother and sisters weep.

Did the soldiers (pilots of bomber planes)
of the Holy city (that flew from the Holy city)
know that they were
to destroy this precious child of Barja?
Our mother and sisters weep.

The militia-man lifts up the boy from the rubble
upon where a high sun throws shadows.
He sees bricks and blocks (slabs of heavy concrete)
struck by missiles (bombers)
controlled by Gorgon, gorilla or people
who slaughtered this nine year old,
a corpse now.
Our mother and sisters weep.

The militia-man realizes, that he too, unwittingly
is accountable for the profanity,
the desecrations on life,
war and anarchy.
Our mother and sisters weep.

Gomer & Spinoza

Wine both new and old is robbing
you of your senses.

Israel and Samaria have turned their back on me,
faithless as Gomer was with Hosea.

I will take her into the desert
and win her back with words of love.

Your love disappears from me
as quickly as morning mist.

You Israel and Judah, souls in alienation,
are condemned by your lies and deceit.

Like a lion I will devour you on the spot.
But I will bring my people back to me.

Like an evergreen tree
I will be the source of all their blessings.

I will be your North and your South,
your sky and your sea, my lover-woman.

Newton, the heliocentric, realized
the clockwork universe, defined laws
of calculus, gravitation and motion.

Spinoza ground lenses
and saw Good
everywhere:

all is Good.
He polished lenses,
observed humanely,

saw the unimportance of problems
sub specie aeternitatis and came to terms
with not being free. *Q.E.D.*

O, holy martyrs and scribes
of the holy books,
assist me in the writing of this canon.

Octavia

Octavia dragged amethyst stones from Mutton Island.
She gathered dale wreck from Diamond Strand.
She knows high or low tides
by the damp and dryness of lapis lazuli stone
she picked on South Strand.
She knows also when the big storm
trapped fish on high sands.
Purple beetroot seaweed, soft wet backwash,
is awash for the woman in magenta clothes.

They ate periwinkles,
drank spring-water
and saw dreamer's archipelago,
where children hunt clandestine crabs
in rock-shallow ponds.

Octavia, the woman dressed in turquoise clothes,
wrote on the rose quartz stones.
O temptress,
for only in the submission to tide-talk,
Octavia knows and that to leave alone in a ship
on the wild and high seas
is sometimes the only imrama.

for Rachel in Besançon, ville natale de Victor Hugo

Jour du Seigneur, jour de dévastation.
Le soleil et la lune s'obscurcissent.
        Il est proche.

Verlaine shot Rimbaud in a quarrel.
Baudelaire found beauty and the ideal
in a hideous world and travelled to Italy
disappointed and depressed.

Les Fleurs du mal —
seized by the police.
Le spleen de Paris —
his alchemy and transfiguration.

Descartes

"You are a wall out of line."
I will forget your evil
deeds.

I will bring my people — Arabs
and Jews — back to their lands
and restore their souls.

The physiologist, Descartes,
certain of the eternal spirit
died of pneumonia

because of the five hours long philosophy class
taught at five a.m. to the Queen of Sweden.
Cogito ergo sum.

Mother of Mercy made the stars,
the Pleiades and Orion.
She is my mater.

Galaxies 31

The Mother of galaxies will judge all nations.
You should not have gloated.

The people of Jacob and Joseph
will be like fire.

They will possess the land that is theirs
by right. He and She shall be King and Queen.

Leibniz of Leipzig,
Dr. Pangloss himself,
devised his calculating machine.

There were truths of reasoning
and truths of fact. The soul
is mirror of an indestructible universe.

Go to Church and hear Cara O'Sullivan, Regina Nathan
and Suzanne Murphy touch our souls. Sirin Vocal ensemble
heal and Mícheál Ó Súilleabháin celebrates.
David Geaney is Lord of the Dance, steps and skates.

Jonah & Coleridge

As Jonah did, I fled to Spain
to avoid the responsibilities
of the word.

I realised that despite our anger
and despair, our clement and concerned mothers saved
120,000 of the Horn of Africa's children.

Like the unrequited Coleridge,
I am the ancient mariner, am
thrown overboard and tell my story.

The Watch

I will walk about barefoot, naked and in sorrow,
howl like a jackal and wail like an ostrich
for we are ruined completely.

We twist and groan. We are besieged. It is hopeless.
All is corrupted. I will watch for thee.
I wait confidently for my Mother's counsel.

Work miracles for us, O father of faith. You will be merciful
to us once again. You forgive us. We will live to see you save us,
O Mother of Hope. Listen, O you hills. We will live in peace.

Be a shepherd to your people.
You will trample our bloated misconceptions underfoot
and send them to the bottom of the sea.

Daughters Pity Us   34

Nahum inveighs
against Nineveh.
O our daughters pity us.

Who can escape your judgement?
Nineveh like Thebes falls
into a drunken stupor.

Chariots flash like fires.
The lion filled his den with torn flesh,
corpses piled high without number.

I can talk with you about imagined dangers,
my own personal daughters,
for you make me complete and with laughter engender.

Art

The sun and the moon stood still
at the flash of your speeding arrows
and the gleam of your shining spear.

But those who are righteous will live because they are faithful.
I, like Habakkuk, shall still be joyful and glad because you
are my saviour and give me strength.

And art can also reflect reality as a mirror —
Rembrandt in a self-portrait and Vermeer's
"Girl reading a letter at an open window".

Liberal and practical Locke
was the sympathetic man. Berkeley held
a Bermudan dream. Love our women.

Sceptical David Hume reflected on reasons, passions
and morals and Hume said custom is the arcane guide.
The Whig Burke created the Tory.

Chapel choirs sang out canon. The blind Landini
composed madrigals. De Machaut's Mass is the oldest
we have and Dufay celebrated *Mass of the armed man.*

Awatiñas, Maraca and Monina Paz dance us — Tango with
    a story.
Michael McCaughan, Barbara O'Shea, Denis Mahood, and
Denis Greig sail our boat across the world in Homage to Paper.

But wait. Sing and shout for joy.
You have ended your punishment.
Play your harps. Play alone, mother.

Zephaniah sings — We are with you.
Polyphonic mastersingers sing out
carols, lieder and chansons.

Gibbons, Tallis and Byrd sing mellifluously
for the Church of England.
Rabelais and Shakespeare rhyme.

Drake and Colombus circumnavigate the globe;
Copernicus and Gallileo
describe the earth rotating round the solar system.

Voltaire ends the *ancien régimen*.
He taught, non-violently enlighten
— view everything in the light of reason.

Free man and free woman are now in chains,
noble and alienated savages, Rousseau cried — Liberty,
Equality, Fraternity. Pray for us, my mother.

Palestrina, director of music in the Sistine
chapel, published a hundred
renaissance Masses for six voices.

Beauty always illuminates
as Michelangelo draws us
to the stories crafted on the Sistine chapel.

Art III

for the Brosnan sisters, Doonties

Dúirt an Tiarna le Hagai —
ón lá seo amach cuirfidh mé
mo bheannacht oraibh.

Kant with wilful intent proved order
in a transcendental world of chaos.
Wagner professed art as did Schopenhauer

who saw art as the only escape
from an irrational world,
our compassion the basis of ethics and love.

Dubliner, John Dowland,
sang from the soul
Lachrymae — flow my tears, *semper dolens.*

IMMA bring us gifts of unresolved art. Alphastates get
us to prance. Craic na Coillte paint 150 year old famine streets
green, blue and yellow. Gurdev Singh plays the magic sarod.
Gerald Barry prepares his tranquil Cahir Waterworld.

Canann Mairianna Nic Ulraig agus Seán Ó Héanaí
le Máiréad agus Tríona Ní Dhomhnaill go gleoite.
Beir bua go deo le Dafydd Iwan, Sliabh Notes agus Kila.
Éist le filíocht álainn, chruinn Mháire Mhac an tSaoi.

The Humble King

Wail and weep oaks of Bashan.
Listen to the roaring of the lions.
An angel riding a red horse followed by
red, dappled and white horses
tells of a helpless and subdued world.
My Brother will help Jerusalem,
Baghdad and New York again.

Four hammers will destroy the four horns of Plenty.
The seven lampstands, the seven eyes of father
and mother, observe all over the earth and seas.
We will live and help Baghdad and New York again.
Look, Zechariah, your future king and his genial mother
come riding on a donkey. Hi to Lisa and all the Muellers in
Miss Fry Drive, Providence. God bless you Mali and America.

Virgil

Ghabh an Macabaech Iarusaileim mí na Nollag 164 r.c.
Bhuail "an Casúr"
Antioheas IV ar a bholg.

The triumvirate is formed by Caesar
with Pompey and Crassus in 60 B.C.
Virgil pens the foremost story of veritable Aeneas
and his remarkable women.

Jack Mapange sings of Malawi where Mags Riordan
runs her lakeside clinic. Praise to her and Fr. Tommie Lynch
where cobra hisses beside his healing Indian Ashram.
Alfred, Boombaya and The Bessa Band play Ghana
          high music Gone jazz.

The Anointed One Is Here

Those who obey Moses' teachings
will be as free and as happy
as calves let out of a stall.

Our Father's and Mother's saving power
will rise on us like the sun
and effect healing like the sun's rays.

Our Brother's day is coming. We will
be His people. He will be our very own.
The Day of the Anointed One is here.

Matthew

My mind is troubled by tax returns,
figures and percentages,
ill at ease and in need of rest.

Caravaggio's *St. Matthew* shows
the evangelist manuscript the word
on the blank page at his desk.

I, Matthew, retire from my accountancy
and career of fraud.
"To remain honest — that is the test."

Mark

He broadcast the sacred
and ever-living
message of eternal salvation.

Mark wrote the story
in 60 A.D., translated Peter's
Aramaic into Greek text.

"I swear that I am telling the truth,
may I be punished if I am not.
I do not know the man." "Desist".

Carracci paints "The Virgin mourning
Christ." Our advocate, Mary,
dispels our deep distress.

The Three Marys

The Three Marys,
Mary, mother of the first son, Jesus,
Mary, mother of James and Joseph
and Mary Magdalene, exorcised of seven devils —
to whom He first appeared,
saved me from perfidy.

And unreasoning sin has drawn me
with real remorse again to do Good.
Jamais, never again will I lose
the sanctifying grace —
knowledge of the Law of Life,
evil and grace.

Loss of respect is the only death, ever.
I hung my head in shame.
But one hundred year old Abraham,
who fathered Isaac,
Moses of the red cow,
King David, the harpist,
The Three Marys
and Salome pardoned me.

He will come with the Three Marys
and with many thousands of His
holy angels
when my soul is tested,
resolve, *jamais*, never again
will I renounce
the Helper, the Holy Spirit.
I accept my life, my death
and my resurrection,
then live for the second.

An Bhreith

Do Mary O'Sullivan, Baile'nranaigh

An Bhreith

A Mháire, tú torrach, ag súil le breith 's
lán de lúcháir,
mar rugadh leanbh do Eiliosaibet freisin.

Tá an Iarúsailéim dubh le daoine.
Ach ní fál go haer é....
Téimis go pluais faoin spéir réaltach.

Síleann an sruth fola. Tá tú i
dtinneas clainne anois. Osclaíonn na sreabhainn. A Mháire,
saolaítear leanbh na Biáide.

Gloria, Gloooria sna harda, in uachtar neimhe,
slua aingil ag moladh Dé ar chnoic, 's an ghealach faoi ré.
Gloria, Gloooria sna harda.

The Birth

Mary, are you content and comfortable?
You are joyous — Elizabeth has borne John,
you're almost at term.

We forge on by Jerusalem, where many
groups convene. We pace to the star-lit cave
on the city's outskirts.

The show trickles. Frequent contractions return.
Membranes rupture. My woman gives birth.
The new-born babe King is delivered.

Gloria to God in the highest heaven —
a great army of angels sings
in the moon-bright hills.

John — James' brother and Mary's Son —
John probably closer to Him
than any other.

You witnessed the transfiguration —
saw Moses and Elijah talk with Him.
He talked with you, James and Peter.

I am the Bread of Life, The Light for the world,
The Word, The Way, The Truth, The Victim,
The Life, The Resurrection and The Viaticum.

Christmas in Mount Mellary, Cappoquin. 2004
For Fr. Tom Lynch, Dhyan Ashram, India.

Welcome, immigrants to Mount Mellary.
Come, St. Benedict calls you good women and
men to our simple and austere lives.

We shall celebrate Christmas with you.
Thrushes exult in wooded Cappoquin. Transport
branches of red-berried holly in the trailer of the
        blue tractor.

Play wind and string instruments in our solitary
Abbey and grey house, where you visit. Again
glorious Mellary becomes alive with angel-song.

Dear immigrants, likewise, you invite us,
indebted now to you, into your lives —
your yellow, brown and bronzed faces smile.

Trumpets announce the Birth of our Immigrant King.
A hundred, thousand welcomes to you, this Christmas.
Bless our world with peace, food, health and song.

Nollaig i gCnoc Mellary, Ceapach Choinn, 2004

Tiomnaithe do Bhreandán Mac Gearailt

Fáilte, a theifeacha, go Cnoc Mellary.
Tagaigí!! Glaonn Naomh Benedict oraibhse, a fhir agus
    a mhná córa
isteach inár saol simplí, aonrach.

Ceiliúraimid an Nollaig libh. Tá na smólaigh ag canadh iomann
i gcoillte in aice Cheapach Choinn. Gearraigí anuas géaga
    de chuileann
na gcaor dearg. Iompraigí é ar an taracóir gorm.

Seinnigí ceol uirlisí aeir agus téad inár mainistir
cumhach agus inár dtigh liath ina bhfuil sibh ar cuairt.
Beidh Mellary arís lán de cheol na n-aingeal.

A theifeacha córa, cuireann sibhse fáilte, romhainn —
sinne faoi fiacha libhse, anois — isteach in bhur saol le bhur
n-aghaidheanna buí, óir, agus dubh-ghorm is bhur ngáirí
    díograiseacha.

Séid an Stoc. Rugadh ár Rí Inimirceach.
Céad míle fáile romhaibh um Nollaig. Beannaigh ár
ndomhan le sláinte, bia, síocháin agus amhráin.

The Quay Wren

for Antanette, Libby & Ann

The Quay Wren marched round
the rain-drenched town.
"Oh that's the banner that Poggin repaired,"
Chris Courtney announced.

Maurice and Jimmy Donegan raised it aloft.
Their father David danced the ancient reel.
The Brosnans, The Griffins, The Keanes, Ó Neachtains
    and The Fannings
dressed in regalia, straw hats and identity concealed.

Eleven whistles played marching wren tunes in the key of C.
The straw for the headgear originated in Co. Meath.
All the boats were tied up. But green and white
drums roll to the constant motion of the sea.

Beat the booming drums young Jason. Brendan, Des,
Tom the Gabha and John Moore thumped the side-drums well.
Con blew the whistle to the meeting of wrens —
music of Fergus's Green and Gold, John St. and the Quay.

Sweet was the sound of music and rain it poured in deluge,
Sarah Brosnan acclaimed — we played the best music on the day.
Pints flowed. Souls grew wild and calm.
She whispered in his ear — "O come with me, my love,
    back the Quay."

Captain John Griffin and his wife of the Quay Wren
had the final say, "God bless The Quay and all you
other wrens," who marched round the streets of the possessed
and sacred towns of Dingle and An Daingean this day.

Saul

Who persecuted and murdered
infidels? Saul later Paul —

raven-haired, pointed nose,
bowlegged, large eyebrows, slight and swarthy.

But he saw the light as would Charlemagne
the writing on the wall.

Paul travelled on board ship
from Palestine, Crete, Greece and Turkey,

shipwrecked in Malta,
then sailed on to Rome.

Pompeii buried in 79 under Vesuvius —
covered every house and wall.

Charlemagne & Gregorian Plain Song

Faith is the beginning, and love is the end —
thought Ignatius of Antioch.
Polycarp chose death as a martyr
was burned at the stake. Constantine ruled supreme in 325.

Augustine from Hippo, published 240 books, born in 354.
Jerome published the Hebrew Bible into Latin,
after 40 years' toil, in 414.

65 emperors ruled Rome
for four hundred years,
in 455 Rome was sacked and forlorn.

The Pope crowned Charlemagne in Rome
Christmas day 800, Holy Roman Emperor,
his chanted word carried further in Gregorian song,
sound floats on the waves of soul.

For four hundred years they sang plainsong
in squat, Romanesque churches. In Milan, the Ambrosian
rite and the Gregorian sang in Rome.

Nóirín and I listen to the plain-chant
on the CD player as we drive over Conor Pass
to walk the silk long strands of Maharees to Derrymore.

Inisfallen's Lepers

for Dr. Dave Hickey

We row to Inisfallen, Island of Faithliu
and of acclaimed beauty.
There is peace in the evening as we sing on the lake.

Monks of St.Augustinian Monastery
of St.Mary, Inisfallen,St.Antony of Egypt and
St. Michael of Sceilg intercede.

We pay homage to you, Mary.
Bless our noscomium for lepers, dedicated to Fionán.
Birds take off over the still lake.

My son Peter visited Peru where the Incas,
divine masters, payed homage to the sun.
There, Che Guevara's lepers were appeased.

Hildegard of the Rhine

Hildegard of Bingen,
poetess on the Rhine and her fifty nuns
sang seven offices daily,

sang hymns to the virgin —
praise the virgin,
source of all fertility.

Teaching, preaching,
Hildegard, the sibyl of the Rhine,
died in 1179.

Kant

Kant fused metaphysical Plato
and polymath Aristotle,
man of the golden mean.

Man is a political animal and woman also!
Kant — we have free will and know that god
exists — the categorical imperative.

Leibniz thought the soul indestructible
as the universe. Doctor Locke believed,
he was a man of common sense, a realist.

Art IV

Shakespeare's drama-poems
staged during the plague
inspire our tender lives.

Shelley rhymed the moral of Ozymanidas.
Victorian troubled and sad Tennyson
mourned King Arthur.

The other notables — human Austin and Dickens —
so also The Brontës and George Eliot
were divine diarists and wordy women. Dostoyevsky,
Pushkin, Gogol, Tolstoy and Turgenev record.

They were good humoured as always —
Tupman, Winkle, Snodgrass and Pickwick,
I heard them laugh. Out of trauma and truth
Dickens said — fiction is born.
Van Gogh claims: "the sadness will never end."

We breathe oxygen and nitrogen of the air.
The planet earth orbits the sun.
Gallileo's father invented recitative.

Handel wrote operatic mass — The Messiah,
the sublime oratorio written in three weeks.
Steinbeck witnessed The Winter of Our Discontent.

Johann Sebastian Bach, violinist in Weimar,
wrote a cantata daily,
wrote for instrument also,

worried about money,
fathered twenty children,
fun-loving, fumbling and spiritual. RE-JOYCE.
We recall Mahfouz's Cairo.

The Robust Family

for The Fanning and O'Farrell Families

I cry — daddy.
In all things my father works for those who love him.
I have peace through my steadfast brothers.

I am put right through my faith in my mother.
Attire in fancy dress. Beat the drums.
I may believe and love at last, sisters.

Hegel

Do Éamonn Ó Neachtain

Mozart, father of classical music,
made the concerto his own,
composed his requiem and died aged 36.

Schelling inspired the repentant
mariner,
Coleridge, to confess.

Hegel, the father Prussian
statesman, on his journey
to self awareness —

Marx and Hitler were nurtured by him.
Kierkegaard condemned
the state idealist. O women save us.

Here I win and lose redemption,
develop my *zeitgeist* and
sip drinking chocolate.

Changed, I acclaim the synthesis.
I am the dialectic.
I am forgiven. I forgive, mother.

Descant of Co. Meath

They excursed to Newgrange,
where on the winter solstice
the sun shines through Boyne passage tomb,
also Knowth and Dowth.

She is the Celtic Love Queen in a chariot of Tara fame.
She encountered the many beloved men to tame,
the brehons, druids, pipers and chess-players. She viewed
all around to Slane, where Patrick fanned the flame.

The Harpers played — Love's fire
is the current of life.
Love's thoughts cannot be quenched,
nor quelled the flash of strife.

They came to Christian Kells
he, to save his loss,
envisaged the church, round tower and
the Book of Kells' eight circle cross.

The Normans dismounted at Trim from France,
the castle secure with
moat and bailey, made Trim
the Royal capital of Tournament and Dance.

Wounded King Billy and James II
fought the Battle of the Boyne
three hundred years later the Boyne
courses through fecund Co. Meath.

Jonathan Swift apotheosised
Stella and Vanessa, both,
who had to ask him;
"Do we love you or loath?"

Ledwidge knows the cry
of vicarious love or loss
for Elsie Vaughan, who was
forbearing and bore her cross.

"Love that is pure is the cream rosebud,"
John B. O'Reilly, Fenian, wrote.
But sometimes love
or the obverse prevaricates the oath.

On a clear night, love can reach
wherever the waves break over
and beneath shores of the moonlit Royal Canal.
Lovers pledge and conceive in Co. Meath.

Catholic Henry V beat the French
at Agincourt
but Joan of Arc was victorious
at Orleans.

Luther translated it into German,
Tyndale bestows on us the English New Testament.
Ó Fiannachta published An Bíobla Naofa
and wins for us grace.

Christians smashed the Turks at Lepanto
in 1571. Japan invaded Korea.
The Black Death ravishes Europe.
England and France fought for a hundred years.

Music finds release from the pain of existence.
Schopenhauer and Wagner cast a spell
on Nietzsche, who cried out Art
for Art's sake.

Forefathers and Mothers, I assert myself
to answer the challenge of myself, to love.
I dare to live and participate in the St. Patrick's Day parade!

Nietzsche drove Mussolini, Hitler and also Bismarck.
Brave man — he was no Nazi. The Superman went insane —
poor man, poor soul, noble soul.

As Hobbes, 1, 2, 3, here I go.
I am about to take my last voyage,
a remarkable leap in the dark.

Mortal will be changed into immortal,
Síóg, the white labrador also.
I shall visit China's Great Wall, that is
5600km long and 10metres high, later this year.

Paul & Shakespeare

I have been given 39 lashes by the Jews and
have been whipped by the Romans three times.
I am in constant danger from false friends.
I was stoned. I have been in three shipwrecks
immersed in the water for twenty-four hours.

Change the world — shouted Marx.
The logical world is horrible — chained Russell,
the mathematician, asked — what are we saying?

Shakespeare, help us make sense of the world
in which we live for a day. The spirit is our freedom. *Om.*
Our women save us again, yet again.
Three cheers — Hip. Hip. Hurrah!

Bantry Estate
for Nóirín

Nóirín arrives here from the fruit-filled orchard
before I behold her in the distance.
She walks between the trees in the country estate.

   Boats roll in the bay.
  The flowers and shrubs bloom,
    irises glow in the park.

Two conflate souls float in our Hegemony,
    when the bees swarm
and the sun, an orange ball, quivers in the sky.

   Nóirín moves deeper
    into the Bantry wood
   under the trees' penumbra.

Cupid & Venus

for Nóirin

I loved a truthful Longford man,
James Martin Clarke.
We were with the fairies —
stars that set-danced in the dark.

Mary McCarthy is my name. I wore a long wool-coat,
and was tender as the moon and gay.
We drifted with the wind on the diamond
stones of Seafield, fresh with sea-spray.

I was as true as any poet that
penned verse by night and day,
that my love for him was unwavering
as the surging surf on the swelling bay.

My laugh is sure and so warm and
continuously we pardon each other.
I sing of my love for James,
in sweet song after sweet song.

Goddesses and Gods of Love, protect us, I scan,
that our lives may be carefree for the day.
From Cupid and Venus I importune to walk
with James, my boon friend, along the windswept bay.

Parliament of Construction.

Apollyon's rule —

Abaddon's Pogrom:
the specious edict.

We are dismembered
in our villages.

We have our souls
by the hasps.

We should come to some
sort of disburdenment

before all marrow
is sucked up in hate.

Then the sun shone
and a most beautiful rainbow
bowed across the heavens.

Cockle Shell Road

for Pádraig, Maura, Breandan and Paul

Under oath I will not
perjure.

I am the defence
and the prosecution.

I wish that I was sworn in
and still laugh at my evidence
so that you could sentence me

any way you wanted
to jeremiadian or Apollonian lands.

At least it wouldn't have been lies.
No hara-kiri either.

Molly and Kathleen laugh.
Live and let live.

Your sentence — walk Cockle Shell road
to the Point.

Listen to the oyster-catchers whistle and cry.
Look — the gurgling Brent geese rise out.

Binnbán Billows

I shall go down to observe
the billows ... loving mermaids will not call me
to dance with the waves.

The billows came roaring down
on Septimus Warren Smith
when he was 30 years of age.

But I am riding a roller-coaster of humiliation,
revenge, jealousy,
affronted by conceit, deceit and effrontery —
an attempt to annihilate me with lies, hate and disdain.

Fe fi fo fum
I love an Englishwoman, Virginia Woolf.
We acclaim the oomph of life.

And the honourable living
descry for glory and honour
from their grave lives.
I honour you anyway.

The billows shall wash away our omissions.
Mermaids will call us all and Mrs. Dalloway
to whoosh with the waves.

Freedom

for Colin, Irene and Aideen

If you sow from the spirit
you will harvest eternal life.
Otherwise you will gather
the mediocre harvest.

We are put right with our father
through our faith in the immortal spirit.
Freedom is what we have mother,
brother, sister and lover.

Manhattan island is sold to the Dutch
for $24, paid in trinkets and beads
and the English named it
New York after the Duke's brother.
Live with oomph wherever.

We are brought from death to life
through our mother's grace.
How broad, long,
deep and wide is our father's love.

Divine Dante and Dostoyevsky call out for their abbé.
Wake up, sleeper, and rise. Get up.
Carry faith as a shield and Fate will shine on you.
Our abbé puts all things under His son's feet.

Great Aquinas echoed Aristotle —
Aquinas, the "dumb ox",
became "the angelic doctor".

Ludwig Wittgenstein — his three brothers dead
by suicide: his famous brother — the pianist
lost his right hand — philosophy as public language.

Still mother's love makes the difference, sometimes diffidence.
Lauren, Con, Stefan and Danny examine the Chagall prints
with indifferent deference.

Heidegger says we face a life of guilt and anxiety.
We scream — to comfort or be comforted
in a universe without glory. But Pegasus saves the day.

Resistance, Resurrection, Liberation —
his triptych — Chagall celebrated the Revolution.
The existentialist, Kierkegaard, believed in the All-Holy.

Eisegesis
for Batt

My room sleeps opposite the Church of The Holy Name.
The air of Christ currents the gothic chapel's
demeanour of Rose window and grey-blocked spiral turret.
Poeta iam domum venit.

I lived with Palladium, a denizen and demimonde.
The wind flows round the Holy Spirit's Yard. Mary blesses
me, this crass and excluded Sufferer with limited lexicon.

I shall fall again but be comforted as I read my eisegesis.
Town sexes the poet of palinodes, he is out of sex and sorts
and yearn passes. The confession palliates bitter remorse.

Light pellucid. A host of sparrows reflects across Murano glass.
Bells resonate twenty times. At Advent, Mary Magdalene calls
vicarious heroes and heroines to Holy Communion
in the transept. So now we're all OK!

Tea in Raffles, Singapore

I should now have the righteousness
that comes from my *beau père*,
and is based on faith. Thanks Pá, thanks son!

England and France war in North America.
East India Company trades in opium and tea.
The Spinning Jenny transforms the work place.

Slaves are traded for tobacco and rum.
France celebrates Bastille Day in 1789.
The 1813 winter defeats Napoleon.
Peter and I partook of tea in Raffles of Singapore.

"Love builds a heaven in Hell's despair."
Comfort us, kind Blake,
who said thus — "What seems to be, is"— our revolution.
We'll travel to Raffles again, my son.

Cassandra Fedele

Frederick William Burton was a seminal soul — No. 3 C
on Yeats' table of the four faculties, and aged 54,
when he painted Cassandra Fedele in her red blouse.

Cassandra was a deserted wife. She boated round
Venice daily for seven years in search of her long lost son.
She was comforted by Gregorian chant.

Her lust was quenched by her torrential
fall of tears all these years.
O my son, why all this unease?

Her son also abandoned Cassandra for years
of self-abandonment. But Cassandra remained
faithful in her crypt of tears.

In a sense she was no. 27 (the saint)
on Yeats' table of the four faculties.
Truth lives. The soul must find her peace.

Our father and mother brought everything on earth and heaven
back to themselves
through their son's sacrificial death at the cross-roads.

Herbert sings — the virtuous soul will live.
Great Milton made a Paradise of hell
with blank verse a bell.

Wordsworth, Shelley, Keats and Byron
romance us to our loves and graves.
Beauty and Art also save.

The Victorian Tennyson sang
"more things are wrought by prayer".
Hopkins sprung rhyme to The Logos.

Emily's 2000 — epigram economy.
Anaïs Nin's essays clarify — commenced with nothing,
connected to the world, and became the artist.

Filí na filíochta siollaí, An Amhráin, An Roisc,
Filí na linne seo, scríbhneoirí na n-Ánnála
's na n-oileán, fan linn anois agus arís. *

And I call on The Mediator and Ultimate Translator
to help me script the epic poem —
commencing in the womb, stopping and starting at the grave.

* Gaelic poets of syllabic and accented metres, contemporary poets,
The Annals' authors and Blasket Island writers, stay with us ever and again.

Daniel O'Connell's Bust at Carhan

53

for John O'Donoghue T.D.

I watch with the chirping wren and the stately heron
the ruins of the birth-house of Daniel O'Connell in Carhan —
my private pilgrimage to our man of world peace.

The kingfisher flies low and swift
blue flash down the turn of stream,
where Carhan river flows to the sea.

There will be the shout of the command,
the archangel's voice, our mother's whisper
and the sound of the Advocate's counsel.
Carhan river flows to the sea.

Carhan, Caherciveen, Co. Kerry

Medicus

For Conor & Jim Brosnan, Finbar & Margo O'Sé and Fíona Kavanagh;
the staff of ILAD, Ionad Leighis an Daingin,
Dingle Hospital, Primary Care, and Dingle Ambulance team and Pat Hanafin

Keep your roots deep in the Word. Your union with woman
frees you from the power of the frightening self.

Now I retire to my book-filled room
where I am surrounded by the world's exalted canons.

Some have passed this way so sad, depressed,
others N.A.D. and some have had no chance at all.

Some of us are sent into the world
to heal, nurse and care,

to physic, smile, do our small share and comfort
in a marasmic world, sometimes out of breath —
tachypnoeic, dyspnoeic and apnoeic.

We'll cure you — every bit
of you and every one of you,
as best we can, and we thank you for entrusting us with you!

We Pay homage to you.

Medicus (Latin) — Healer

Dick Mack's

purveyor of dreams

This is a pantisocracy
for you, men and women drinkers
of Dick Mack's.

No Panglossian fool here, no, no, nor anyone
pulverised by pretence. Purchase your boots
and leather straps in Dick Mack's.

Under Dick Mack's bust
you are privy to a party of non-smokers
and social anti-social drinkers.

You meet your daughters, sister,
mother, Oliver Mack, Gene Courtney
and the Goddess holding court.

Love-music brings you with friends
agape, to face the early morning
under St. Mary's cold grey steeple.

"The first time ever I saw your face."
Love, joy and self-respect
fill the town and last forever.

You will encounter fellow cheerful
travellers and dreamers in Dick Mack's.
Caveat: beware of Dick Mack's ghosts.

Huany ing ni / Welcome

International Physicians for the Prevention of Nuclear War (IPPNW)
World Conference, Beijing, 2004

Life is pleasant in Beijing
walk the Great Wall, 5600km long,
10 metres high in Badilin,

on to Simatrai through
magical villages and communes
silver-glimmering.

Horse's head Qin recital
with Mei Li Yin Yue Hui.
Blow bamboo flutes and sheng.

Take an afternoon stroll
in the jasmine Summer Palace
with Fíona and Nóirín.

Advance bravely. Kang Ding Qing Ge.
People call, *Ní Háo.*
How are you in Tian'amen?

Xiexie. Thank you.
Good-bye. *Zaijian.*
Bicycle bells ding-a-ling.

Rise Out, My Love

Feed yourself spiritually on the words of faith.
What did we bring into the world? Nothing.
What can we take out of the world? Nothing.

Hell is other people, thought Sartre. Hell, surely!
Simone de Beauvoir found worth.
Camus considered — life, the absurd.

Famine devastates China.
Boers assert themselves as do the Irish.
Europe partitions Africa and thieves.

King Leopold exploits the Congo.
The Wright brothers take to the air.
Amunsden reaches the South Pole.
We travel on the Darjeeling railway.

Run your best in the race of faith.
Win eternal life for yourself. We're all winners!
Command all to place hope in our mothers.

Rise out, my love. Clare and Kevin
sing Neruda's love hymns
together, Love — *El Amor*.
Joan Baez ballads — til my days are gone.

Sacred Books

Loyal soldier of Love, I remember your tears.
Do not forget to bring my coat that I left in Troas with Carpus.
Bring the books too, especially the ones made of parchment.

Keep away from foolish and ignorant arguments.
Our new history begins with the resurrection. Preach the
message of the good news and we will be put right with the
Queen and King of Glory.

My Father and Mother, the saints,
authors of tens of thousands of texts,
and all the angels came and lifted this canon —

not an *argumentum ad populum* nor deliberative oratory
but for this essential definition of the soul
and its intention. Let's hope it sells well. Buy another copy.

All authors in heaven lifted the text
at the consecration of the Lamb
and gave it its blessing to heal us when we hate.

Lux perpetua luceat eis.
Bless all — Krishna, Krishna, Hari, Hari,
great spirit of Buddha and Allah.

Byblos
for Ruth

I read sixty-six books of Byblos,
also, one hundred and fourteen
Suras of Allah by the Mediterranean sea.

Moslems build minarets in new mosques.
The calligraphy of the Koran
illuminates Allah's text.

The Israeli planes broke
the sound barrier.
The helicopters flew in a pair
over Byblos.

However, the Moslems, Christians and Jews —
men and women — all parade on the Cornice by the sea.
The chartered planes fly overhead,
one every five minutes, into Beirut airport.

Hoovering

for Rita and Eddie

57

Show a gentle attitude towards everyone.
The poet recovers from a hell of a headache,
feeds the cats, Síóg our white labrador,
and empties the dishwasher.

O Domine, libera
animam meam.
May The Lord and Mary keep my soul.

I hoover the room,
prepare the breakfast, coffee and eggs,
care for the eternal aged,
praise more than blame and have another coffee.

Muragab

To Brian Kennedy

Ten thousand lights flashed
as charms of finches,
tidings of magpies and flights of swallows
crossed the tangled hills.

The thrush she sings on a new spring lime.
Muragab and he, they sleep in the street
where they are alarmed and troubled
in loveless wander, far from Fearthain fields.

He had asked Muragab to send down
a fall of woodcock on this god-forsaken row.
"Of course I shall, my Love,
but of course, before you go."

Muragab, there is love within him despite
cultural, emotional and social discord,
as a murder of crows flies past, while the skein
of geese rush into the green town-park.

Muragab desired him unexpectedly near birch
trees, from where trawler boats depart,
where men and women whisper together
and a parliament of owls hoots for him and Muragab.

Out of the Depths of Beethoven

for Barry Douglas

Forgive me, your slave.
I am now the slave of
my dear brother, The Spirit of Truth.
I return to you, my mother.

Who can compose anything of note
after the romantic music of Beethoven?
Melodious Beethoven railed against the heavens.
The 9 symphonies announced the birth of a whole New World.

De profundis clamavi ad te.
Domine, Domine, exaudi vocem meam.
Hear my voice, dreamer, Bob Dylan lilts.
I have cried to Thee out of the depths of Beethoven.

Tim

(Easter, April 2004)

Blow the brass.
Tremble the percussion.
Let the strings play.
Sing voices, sing so quiet.

The Dingle Fife and Drum march 6 a.m.
Easter Sunday and Saint Patrick's Day morning.
March up and down the streets.
Tim goes before playing his fife.

Tell our friends — He surely lived
but he is now dead and risen from the dead.
Drink a glass of whiskey
in homage to his life.

Now put on your suit.
Pray for his soul,
the soul of his sweet family
and his loved ones and Joan.

5000 prayed for you.
A Thaidhg, a stór, Cathal and Bert keen.
Pay your respects for Tadhg
who died and rose this week.

Six months later, we think of you often and much —
a man of deep sympathies and lived an honest life.
You returned to your silver shore and enriched us.
The hagiography on St. Francis of Assisi was your parting lore.

O Skipper, glory to You, our friend, Tim.
Blasket seal. Rón an Bhlascaoid. Snámh linn abhaile.
Guide us on our Shannon. Chips and Philip lament.
Direct us to our safe harbour, a Thaidhg. Amen.

Uncertainty

for the Houlihan family, Avondale

The word of our father
and mother is alive and active.
It cuts all the way through to where
soul and spirit meet.

To have faith is to be uncertain.
Everything in all creation
is exposed to Him and Her
and lies at the feet.

*Quia apud Dominum
misericordia: et copiosa
apud Eum redemptio.*

Because with them there
is mercy: and with Him
and Her plentiful redemption.

I'll have another coffee but where — in Penny's
blue and pink tea rooms or in one of Dingle's or An Daingean
or Daingean Uí Chúise' forty cafés and hostelries?

If anybody is happy —
lift up your voice in songs and poems
and withstand the perils of doubt.

A Limerick rake, Desmond, the Wandering celt, O'Grady
listens to Umm Kulthum in an Alexandrian garden and takes
to the road. Glory to them that their exile is prolonged.

Audrey Hepburn enthralls. Leonard Cohen recalls.
Shostakovich no.13 hymns great tall
Yevgeny Yevtushenko's *Babi Yar*.

Johnny Cash, Britney Spears and Shakespear's Sister sing
for my father and mother, the living Good.
A porta inferi erue Domine, animas eorum.
Deliver all souls from the gates of isolation.

Encourage us to sing, shout and dance
lively jigs and Connemara reels.
O Rachel, my daughter, play merrily
on the silver concert flute.
Peter, play the clarinet — The Pink Panther.

Téir an 671km ón mBuailtín go Penstivien.
Seinn an chláirseach Anne Aufret. Séid an Bombard.
Tionlachan Fergal, Louis 's Aoileann. Tagann muintir
Panceltic le Tegwyn. Seineann Aoife, Jon agus Mark
le draíocht. Rinceann ceol Tzigani Live.
Canann Séamas Ó Beaglaoích — Fill, a rún ó, go hÉireann.

(Travel 671km from Ballyferriter to Penstivien. Anne Aufret play the harp. Blow
the bombard. Accompany Fergal, Louis and Aoileann. Our Panceltic family arrives
with Tegwyn. Aoife, Jon and Mark play magically. Tzigani Live delights. Séamas
Begley sings — Come back, my love, to Éireann.)

Come as living stones.
Let yourselves
be used in building
the spiritual temple.

Whoever suffers physically, is no longer lost.
Humble yourself under the Deity's mighty hand in union
with the Divinity, who will himself and herself perfect you,
give you firmness, fullness, a sure foundation and strength.

Bruckner felt overshadowed
by Wagner
eventually wrote his ninth.
Brahms was in love with Clara.

Selig sind, die da leid tragen
Blessed are they that mourn
for they shall be comforted.
Blessed are the dead, that's all of us
within ten, twenty and eighty years.

The Disc-Removal
for Charles Marks

I had run all my life over hill and strand,
covered thirty miles a week on road
and addicted to the endorphin surge.

One evening on the sea-song sand dunes,
in June, the day was long and clear,
the *nucleus pulposous* ruptured the *annulus fibrosus*
pressed on my spinal nerves and fear.

Oh! the pain was five months sciatica long,
day and night, persistent pressed not vicarious
at all, effected pins and needles, numbness,
a vice-grip on right hip, sinister spasm in the car.

Protrusion, impingement, stenosis, migration,
irritation and narrowing — the MRI revealed all.
"Time to start cracking," said Charly Marks,
"if the pain is there, half a year, 'tis a small job after all."

Nothing like God's own non-pretentious public hospital —
aspiring junior staff and nurses, intimate and calm, housekeepers
homely and kind, best wishes from family and fifty friends,
rattling trolleys, B.P. cuffs on wheels and ringing phones.

Mobile conversations and other patients' accounts —
aneurysms to clip, shunt intracranial hypertension,
burr hole extradurals and slow subdural
bleeds due to falls and brawls.

Pituitary tumours, secretory and non-secretory —
I'd heard of in my dissociated, bohemian student days —
tragic stories — why he, she, you, them or me? Today the
    odd tear falls.
Soul defining seconds on this ward. Not maudlin at all.

I am on ward GA with a "minor neurological problem".
The disc patient isn't too bad at all — microdissection L5/S1.
Mike Harris, George Shorten and skillful staff in Recovery,
send me home to put on my socks, swim, heal with physiotherapy,
walk the furze lined hills of Sraidbally and jog the seagull strands again.

Christmas Holiday in Syria

I shall soon put off this mortal body,
righteousness will be at home
under the control of the Paraclete.

Archduke Ferdinand assassinated by a Serb in Sarajevo.
Bolsheviks stage a *coup d'etat.* Allies smash German lines.
10 million dead. Great Damascus is freed.

Gandhi jailed. Marconi Co. broadcast.
Lenin died in 1924.
Peter, Nóirín and I visited his mausoleum.

We lived on hummus in Damascus, digested
literary plots in Aleppo, and dates in Palmyra —
the family made a supreme Christmas holiday
round Syria in 2002.

Yet Scheherazade told
Schahria, the Caliph, tales for 1001 nights
to avoid being beheaded by the mass beheader.

Badralbudur saved Aladdin from envy,
wickedness and the desire for power by
her goodness.
We walked round Aleppo in December.

Bruckner, Tchaikovsky, Mahler & Brahms

Whoever loves his brother
and sister lives in the light
because love comes from the father
and mother.

He who defeats the world
believes that he is
the son of our father and mother.

Naïve Bruckner —
organist with baggy trousers
built a cathedral of sounds.

Bachelor Brahms cared for his mother,
and penned the most sombre of all,
The German Requiem.

Tchaikovsky composed *Eugene Onegin*, a man
who rejects love, until it is too late. Disharmonious
and closet homosexual, after the despairing 6th Symphony,
    he died aged fifty-three.

Penniless Mahler wrote symphony of a thousand voices —
with grief and suffering, he used progressive tonality,
bands off stage — the last of the Vienna symphonists.

Angkor Wat is built by the Khmer for Hindu worship.
A Buddha (Gautama) leaves his home to renounce all
worldly goods and claims salvation for west and east.

Terror launched in Hitler's Germany.
He aids Franco, bombs Guernica
and invades the USSR who defy.

Hong Kong fell to Japan.
"Vive Paris," cried De Gaulle.
Atom bomb wipes out Hiroshima.

U2 incant — disband the atomic bomb.
Miserere mei, sana me, exaudi orationem meam.
Have mercy, heal me and hear my prayer.
Back in the USSR — The Beatles sing.

From Mt. Brandon's crosses we view the Holy Blaskets,
the absolving Skelligs and The Saints' Way.
We splurge through bog, fog, short biting showers
and reach Brendan's cell on the summit.

After tea and fruit we descend on the pilgrimage —
quick steps now, muscles pinch and stretch.
Skin is warm and we return to Danno's for a homecoming
to the Salsa music and song of Germans and Brazilians.
Pauline Scanlon and Donagh sing for us in Brics and McCarthys.

Death Is Our Victory 64

Dear Lady, let us all love
one another. Let us encourage
one another at all times.

Mozart, also Salieri, so also
the Frenchman, Fauré, and the German,
Brahms, sang for the dead.

Blessed are the dead, especially Mick
and Kieran. I do not want to die, decompose,
be nibbled by rats, but I must expect to soon.

Into thy hands I shall commend
my spirit. I shall now embrace the sleep of death
with dreams of slugs, snails and salvation.

Death is our victory, dear Lady,
with the righteous and faithful
in the abode of the blessed. He huffed, puffed
and blew our house down.

In paradisum deducant te angeli.
In tuo adventu suscipiant te martyres
et perducant te in civitatem sanctam, Jerusalem.

May the angels lead thee into paradise.
May the martyrs receive thee at thy coming
and bring thee into the holy city, Jerusalem.

Requiem for Winda 1998–2004 (Indonesia)
for Peter

Sleep, sleep my child, Winda.
Sleep. Rest. Rise up and Dance.
Flower girl, Dance.

Raymond and Selfina
rose our of the sea and
gave birth to Winda, our child —

glorious the occasion on December 15th.
Winda lived in Manado sea gardens.
Winda, our sweet love, our child.

Winda played under canopies of coconut,
ate copra, ice-cream and drank *milu siram*.
Coconut leaves wave in the wind over her garden.

Winda played with Ariel, her brother and
Brino, her pet dog. She swam like a fish in the sea gardens.
Gunung Api, fire mountains, light up the sky-line afar.

Weep for us. Weep for our child,
our Indonesian child.
Sleep our precious one. Weep.

Yolanda reads to Winda.
Red and pink, her colours, on the coral reef.
Winda swims in the sea garden.

Suffering little children,
are we done with our weeping?
Have we cried all our tears?

A debilitating disease struck...
Six years of age the angels call her to take
to her Heaven. Here comes the green car.

Dance forever. Dance
on the mountains of Mollucas.
Dance our loved one forever.

Winda, we'll soon come and join you
but Peace and Pancasila, you shall bring us,
while we wait for our call.

Rise up out of the ashes, dear Winda.
Let us laugh now, please let us laugh.
We shall laugh. Please do not weep at all
— let the wind blow our sorrow afar.

Day of Calamity & Misery

65

Beware you are Diotrephes.
Dies irae dies illa — the bells incant
"Shoulder the poet's coffin to the grave."

Shostakovich wrote the 10th symphony to celebrate
the death of ignominious Stalin. Dresden quartet
was dedicated to the memory of all war victims.

Chorus angelorum te suscipiat
et cum Lazaro quondam paupere
aeternam habeas requiem.

May the choir of angels receive thee, Kieran and Mick,
and with Lazarus, who once was poor,
may you have eternal rest.

Pity us, Jesus Lord.
Pay homage to God,
our fearless, loving Son and his mother, Mary.

Dum veneris judicare
saeculum
per ignem.

When thou shalt come to judge
the world by fire. Quake destroys Bam and Kashmir.
Iran celebrates Ebadi.

Dies calamitatis
et miseriae.
Dies magna et amara valde.

Day of calamity and misery.
That grand day and most bitter.
Solemn bells ring out.

A Eilís, Eibhlín agus Áine canaigí le huaisleacht.
A Mhaidhc Dainín seinn port binn le Tim Edey go déanach.
Eilís, Eibhlín and Áine sing nobly.
Maidhc Dainín plays sweet tunes with Tim Edey finally.

I am supplicant on my knees. Bells incant most solemnly.
O my family shoulder my coffin. Throw roses on my grave
    wherever.
Be steadfast and pay homage to Christ Almighty and Mary
and to us consoled children of Patrick and Bridget.

Tsunami

2005-01-01

326,000 drowned by six waves —
the feared tsunami,
Tambora in 1815 and
Krakatau in 1883.

Now — a plane of water 30 feet high
surges 2,000 miles across Asia — Sri Lanka, Sumatra,
    Thailand, India and Maldives.
Powerful, planned and executed
with deathly precision.

The Sri Lankan priest agreed it would be
difficult to explain God's position,
that is to say, God's Purpose —
if God is responsible for everything
or maybe the Forces of evil sometimes win,
man's inhumanity to man etc. etc.

But if God is complicit why did
God of Good allow this sacrificial slaughter
of 326,000 in an outbursting of nature?
Tragedy on a mass scale, grief, fear and hysteria in Meulaboh.
Strike the gongs, canang, mong-mong and rapai in Banda Aceh.

And I believe God did understand this stench
would shock this unstable world to condole,
bring us to our senses, to forgive, to disarm and to make peace
    or maybe not.

We shall all die, be buried and rise out
eternally from the bowels of the earth or sea.
The world mourns and does not understand.

Gallaras

do Choiste Féile na Bealtaine agus Deirdre Ní Ghrifín

Aireagal Ghallarais.
Gallaras —
Bád iompaithe bun os cionn.

Siúlaim go glórach ar na clocha.
Tá Deora Dé ag líonadh isteach
ar an gcosán.

Mise atá suite os comhair an Aireagail,
mé sásta, foighneach, ag rá iomann atá
ornáideach, grástúil 's mé ag éisteacht ón bhfraoch
le ceol siansach an loin duibh.

Míorúilt na gcloch
os mo chomhair,
Gallaras.

Gallarus

for Joan Rohan and her mother

Gallarus oratory.
Gallarus —
Boat turned downside up.

We walk on squelching pebbles.
Fuchsia,God's tears, flow over
on to the path.

We sit facing the oratory — contented and patient.
We sing hallowed and respectful songs and
listen to the blackbird sing sweetly over the heather.

The miracle of stone
faces us —
Gallarus.

Penultimately —

Homage to Peace

Seventeen poems are composed to the drawings of Marcel Chirnoaga, Bucharest.
Variations on stanza forms are used.

Marcel Chirnoaga   *A1*

Many thanks to you and youthful
St. John, Mary and Daniel, who saw His face
covered in hair, white as wool.

Among seven gold lampstands, His eyes burn like fireball,
a sharp two-edged sword came from his mouth.
His feet like brass, His voice — a roaring waterfall.

My time of glory and sacrifice —
my Apocalypse has arrived.
Let it not be too fearful. Come.

Holy, Holy   *A2*

'Holy, holy, holy,
All-Holy' four
creatures chant the hymnody.

The burnished souls decry.·
The grey crow plucked out
the tongue of the lamb and eye.

The twenty-four elders refrain.
'Our All-Merciful and our radiant
Mother, both of You palliate pain.'

Seal   *A3*

The Lamb cleaved
open seals, as suns
they glow.

The Rider, Robin Cook, on the white
horse, primes the bow, rides
the winner at Dingle Races.

The Rider on the red Horse
wields a sword
to and fro in London and Sharm el Sheik.

The Rider on the Black Horse
jounces *wings of death*,
high and low, rides to Hiroshima.

The warriors devour
horse flesh in
the valley of sadists.

Eight thousand massacred
in one foul ambush
in a Rwandan debacle.

Croats in a pincer jerk
counter response to
a Serb Krijna attack.

The Separatists match a
strike at a Russian plane
in a Chechnya dispatch.

The Riders on the pale horses —
Death and Hades. 9/11 air attack.
Twin Towers collapse.

Iraq disembowelled. Oil and gas depleted — Blair and
Bush ignored UN law. *Caveat.* What can good people every
where do but mourn, protest, pray and fast?

Fifth Trumpet Blower   *A4*

Locusts descended in file
upon earth, scorpions high
as horses beguile.

For five months they defy
and torture the sealless
ones with boils.

Their leader — godless
Abaddon, destroyer
Apollyon, ruthless.

Fallujah destroyed. Baghdad and Mosul under siege.
100,000 civilians suffered death. 1,000 trampled in Baghdad.
Bombs and typhoid burden a country in ruins.

Keep secret what the thunder
noises, takes with guile; men and
women are afeared and torn asunder.

Blow trumpets. Defile.
Expedite Death. None
can escape The Judge's bile.

Witness   *A5*

So that we be not damned,
for forty years we wander in alarm,
the two olive trees, the two lamps
render glory to the Lamb.
Our friends, Brenda, Trish and Simone
exult in Cloghane. Run on Castle beach.
Swim in Tralee bay's green-blue ocean.

Matrix, and dragon *A6*

Her dress the sun,
the moon under her feet,
the stars round her head.

Infant off-spring,
innocent cries —
War in heaven.

May Gabriel, Michael
protect the mothers,
the babes — anointed ones

from the red dragon
of seven heads
and ten long horns,

head-dress of seven
diadems; diabolism,
the Mephisto, beast

seducer, bad Mephistopheles,
vampire — the dragon, but
fearful of the Lamb's mother.

Two Beasts *A7*

the dragon and the vengeful beast with the head of a lion,
the hateful dragon of seven heads and ten crowned horns;
resembling a leopard; six hundred and sixty six, tattooed loin.
Cunning, baffling Lucifer, empowered prince of devils,
ill physically, mentally craving, spiritually bereft,
incites, blasphemes the All-Wise to rally. Apocalypse thirteen;
666, the no. of the beast. Who can escape the Beelzebub's
deception? The Lamb sings hymns to the harp's accompaniment —
Salvé Regina. Deum laudamus. Libera nos a malo.
Give glory to the guardian of Life, strife's Author.
Behold I come. *Ecce venio.*

All *A8*

'Cut from the earth's vineyards all.
Throw the grapes into a winepress. Steep
in Emmanuel's love, laughter and all.'

Rejoicing, I leave the treadmill hall,
sanitising sauna and chlorine leap.
Cut from the earth's vineyards all.

March for the Live 8 Ball. Hear Bono and Paul,
Bob, REM, Pink Floyd, Madonna, and Robbie.
Sing in Emmanuel's love, laughter and all.

The sea flowed for miles. Play GAA rules football
with powerful Páidi, Bernard and Barry. Walk on
Castle beach. Cut from the earth's vineyards all.

Hosanna in excelsis for to Foxy John's we call.
At Nóra's in Ballyferriter we reap
Emmanuel's love, laughter and gall.

It is requisite, right to forgive all.
Recall parks where children peep —
cut from the earth's vineyards all;
Emmanuel's love, laughter and all.

Final Plagues *A9*

The Bowls of Yahweh's anger pour
on the half-living dead.
The Ignominious Frogs we dread.
The three evil spirits roar.

UNICEF pleads for food, water, houses,
education, women's health and peace.
Our World's two thirds deceased.

Loudest thunderbolt,
still no roads' repair,
Beslan's despair,
Disease and Revolt.

Malice is nigh. O women save us.
Ten-stone hail stones propulse space zone
from Dis and High. We ignore South America.
Everywhere AIDS. O women save us.

Star Wars programme expanded.
Multinationals to ruin? Internecine Doom;
New Orleans drowned.
London, New York, Baghdad, and Rome
decapitated, hatred unbounded.
Feed Africa. O women save us.

Agnus Dei qui tollis
peccata mundi
dona eis requiem
sempiternam.

Requiem   *A10*

The abused queen of page three,
one of the famous prostitutes,
discards her scarlet cloak,
frilly lingerie and purple boots.

Traducer of the west and east,
she rides the red beast
of seven heads and
ten horns to the feast.

The carnal beast itself is
the eighth dismal king,
he dismounts to die, all the kings
pardon or will accept the hand of
cards they've been dealt.

May the incessant running
of the waves on the shore-skin
prevent thoughts of temptation, and
atone again our disdainful loneliness.

Dies Irae.
Dona eis requiem.
Requiescant in pace.
Dona eis pacem.

The Fall   *A11*

It is I, Babylon, New York,
Beijing and London, at thirty-six
and a decade later
have fallen so lonesome and foul.

'For all nations have drunk
the immoral wine from her lustful bowl.'
I am hunted by demons, hateful birds echo
Hutu spirits from Kibeho.

Making injustice, state and non-state terrorism and poverty
    history.
Listen to John Liddy read in The Milesians. Visit Derry's
agricultural show. Row in Eddie Hutch's and Maunze's regatta.
Stockwell says, "Concern saved Somalia."

Confutatis maledictis
flammis acribus addictis
voca me cum benedictis.

When the cursed in
anguish flee into
flames of misery,
call me with the blest.

Word of Light   *A12*

Come to wedding feast of the Lamb
and His bride, who heal our hurt.

144,000 call The Rider
on the white horse, — Loyalty, Truth.

Gandhi speaks the force of truth.
Lux Aeterna, Lord of Light and worth.

Following Him his army, south
galloping on white horses North.

Lady Peace and Honour — his bride.
Glory and praise to God Almighty forth.

Anointed One's Great Feast   *A13*

the beast and false prophet are thrown
into the lake of fire. Birds gulp the flesh
of soldiers, riders and kings who groan;
horses and corpses bloodied in a mess.

Lord, embellish our bones and soul,
with interlacing divine benedictions bless.
May the eagles of the All-Wise women console.
May The Anointed One our mortality redress.

Victory   *A14*

For the women angels seized the serpent, demons and fears
locked them in internment for thousands of years.
Please Brother Bertie stop Shannon stopover now. Arrest
Uncle Sam's continuous assault on Iraq. Make Peace for
Shia, Sunni and Kurds and Al-Qaeda too.
British and American pals now please leave Iraq.
Victor is the Lamb, God-sent, woman's *Pharmakos* who forbears.
Jesus Christ's canons illustrate the completed irony of Fate.

Fire and Sulphur   *A15*

Fair Trade, disarm, forgive debts,
drive safely on the roads and pay respect.
The Evil was expelled into fire and sulphur
where the evil beast and the false prophets are tormented
and lonesome for ever and ever.

Book of Life   *A16*

Is my name not in The Book of Living? Well done, El-Baradei.
In the Lake of Fire the soul is healing. We, IAEA, may
travel from An Daingean to Santiago de Compostela in the evening
and wear scallop shells on El Camino for the healing.

New Jerusalem, His Bride   *A17*

God's retribution is past.
He gives us Land and Peace.
Accept His love which lasts.

The city of truth, 1500 miles square,
as wide, and as high as it was long,
shines with the glory of God's care.

New Jerusalem, the lamb's bride,
descended from heaven. The Bride and
The Lamb with us shall abide.

Our mothers have made us attain
and call again the Lamb. Almighty
Love of Good and the lamb sustains.

Tree and Water of Life forgive.
The Foundation stones are forgiveness,
mercy, always death, truth and tears.

Commencement, present, past
and End is with our Good Father and His
Bride. Lord, come home at last.

Antarctica, Himalayas & Torc —
Time for me — myself

for Con Ó Muircheartaigh and Pat Falvey

"Between Weddell and Ross seas
on the summit of Mt. Vinson
in Antarctica, round me a sea of white.
20,000 ft. of ice pushes down the mountains.
Being with me, myself.

Camp 4, at 26,000 ft,
100 mph wind — a raging train on the tracks,
blue tent pitched on the down slope of Everest.
A chain of mountains 2000 miles long.
The Himalayas.

Sherpa Pemba Gyalji
handed me a fossil —
a fish sculpted on stone, pushed by tectonic plates
and forces of our planet,
five and half miles up into the sky —
a world turned down-side up.
Time for me, myself."

On top of Torc
overlooking beautiful Killarney,
we see as far as the Galtees.
Pugin cathedral rests beyond the mirroring lake.
Oh Killarney, where for five years I was schooled.
Time for us — ourselves.

The Train Journey

(from Killarney to Dublin)

The train pulls out,
the light from other villages and towns
highlights the distance.
The Pap Mountains —
black pieces cut out of cardboard boxes
in the brown beyond.
An uneasy bare bush of winter
shakes in the eclipse of light.
Grey mist ascends and a crimson red
tinges the skyline above the fields
that run up and down from the horizon.

Morning has dulled.
Clumsy crows move beside and faraway.
I am absorbed with their actions.
They will procure food against various odds.
A blackbird perches on a fog-filled parish,
a falling snow at Banteer.

People in a farmhouse with lights on
prepare to begin sacrifices to Gods and Goddesses
in regional rituals.
Dung spread in small fields,
forty trailer loads,
work wasted or expended.
Sweat rolls out to evaporate
beyond the zodiac.

*

Twenty cypress trees appear
damp on the borders of zephyr blown fields.
I am desultory.

Look, I see a jocose woman in a wood of conifers
near Thurles. Hide in there in the comfort tunnels
of sunbeams.
Roll in there in green lush herbage.
Hear an ass bray and a horse neigh.
Drink in water from a well and
dwell on the mystery.
Rabbits, hares hop by sniff the wind
and notice a cuckoo spit.
Things, places that appeared real
in times that were
are in layers within an obstreperous will.
Blow oboe, bamboo flutes and sheng.
Blow oboe, as you will,
a giddy arpeggio.

The tea-woman announces —
"I bring you drinks or juices of any sort."
"Do the banks own all?"
asks a politician in polemic discussion.
"Breathe in, breathe out
because you are a liberator of the torts," another proffers.
"Do the banks own me? But they are good employers.
It is inept, this usuric hold," she offers.
She sips her drink while awakening.
Sunlight breaks through clouds beyond
and bursts its light on a Norman castle.
The sun in hide again,
heats a silage pit, anchored
by fifty tyres indefectibly tied.
Light in emboldened effort
outshines its previous magic quiver.
The Sun, a forge, kindling my soul
to activity, to repose, to be pardoned
and to forgive.

*

A brace of pheasant rises.
Two jackdaws fly long distances
near a fence beside a remote field
of seeding furze.
A murmuration of starling flits
past,
acknowledges grey-slow morning
and flouting inner secrets.
Through the cloud a jet courses
to other magical countries.

A Woman walks a grey black field, near Portlaoise.
She vanishes with you in song.
Pipits, you encourage her
with whistling movements and
your consistent calling.
She drifts away.
A slow, serene stream
winds beneath the zenith.

We travel in long carriages,
jolted to and fro,
over and back.
Our screeching yellow train
passes a syntonic station.
We shall come back.
Train floats through the light,
silver carriages on golden tracks.
Thoughts drum into nebula
    and eternal galaxies.
Til we meet again
pax vobis —
peace go with you always.